Honoring the Art of Our Lives

An Interview with Alan C. O'Hare

Dorian Mintzer

ORANGE, TX

Honoring the Art of Our Lives: An Interview with Alan C. O'Hare – Dorian Mintzer. -- 1st ed.
ISBN 9798733568782

The Publisher has strived to be as accurate and complete as possible in creating this book, but some edits were made for readability.

This book is not intended for use as a legal, business, accounting, or financial advice source. All readers are advised to seek competent professionals in legal, business, accounting, and finance field.

Like anything else in life, there are no guarantees of income or results in practical advice books. Readers are cautioned to rely on their own judgment about their individual circumstances to act accordingly.

While all attempts have been made to verify information provided in this publication, the Publisher assumes no responsibility for errors, omissions, or contrary interpretation of the subject matter herein. Any perceived slights of specific persons, peoples, or organizations are unintentional.

FREE GIFT FOR READERS

As a gift for my readers, I have an amazing retirement resources list for you.

Get your copy today at

http://10KeyRetirementIssues.com

Rave Reviews

"Dorian Mintzer is a jewel. In life, it is rare to find people who really care and who listen not only with their ears, but with their hearts. Kind, compassionate, intelligent - Dorian is a gifted coach and consultant. Those who are her clients, associates, and friends are truly lucky to know her. Thank you for being you."

\- Nancy Mills, Founder, The Spirited Woman

"Dorian has been my career coach for over two years, and without her, I would not have been patient enough to finally be employed in 'my dream job.' Originally, I sought out a career coach because I had 'career anxiety,' As an academic and researcher following the usual course of tenure and NIH funding, I was very unhappy. I felt useless, lacking in talent and creativity, and that my current career path was hopeless.

Still, I was surrounded by persons like me who encouraged me to 'stay the course' despite my gut feelings that, for me, it was all wrong. By working with Dorian, I began to let go, explore, examine possibilities, and try these out. I eliminated anger and resentment from my life with her help.

Today, I am utilizing my strengths and skills in a satisfying and fulfilling work environment. I have the social support and team spirit that was lacking. I am intellectually challenged and surrounded by bright people who are passionate about their research and careers. Grant writing and getting tenure have become background 'noise,' and my new focus is to enjoy using my strengths, skills, and talents in preparing for my 'final scene.'

I don't know when that will be because I work every day with passion, enthusiasm, and enjoyment and am beginning to have a personal life again that is void of tension, guilt, and career anxiety. The search for the perfect job as a tenured scientist has ended-today I work with joy and fulfillment. That is all that is needed, not the struggle to achieve another credential or award. Thank you, Dorian and all life transition and career coaches, for what you do!!
- Esther Bay, Ph.D., R.N.

"Dorian was very generous with her time, her knowledge, and her consideration of me. I was going through a prolonged and often frustrating job search/career change process. She helped me through this process by offering various perspectives and by helping me with suggestions and ideas. As a Coach, Dorian seemed to have a good sense of when to provide direction and when to allow room to explore various career possibilities. I am now employed thanks, in large part, to Dorian's coaching expertise. Her professionalism is beyond category."
- Peter Espiefs, Mental Health Counselor at Lahey Behavioral Health Services

"Dr. Dori is the real deal! Her presentation was enlightening and game-changing for a number of our members who specialize in couples and retirement. She has a kind and caring style that made it easy for members to interact

with her, and the time she gave to members after her session made a huge impact. Delivered beyond our expectations. Highly recommended!"

- Robert Laura, President, Retirement Coaches Association

"Dorian, thank you again for your stellar presentation to the Retirement Coaches Association 2018 Conference. Your informative insights continue to resonate with me as I help my clients mentally prepare for the "challenges and opportunities" ahead. You model the best of what retirement coaching can be, and for that, I am grateful."

- Dr. Deborah W. Holton, Associate Professor, DePaul University

"As a certified coach of Retirement Options, I recently had the pleasure of listening in on a call with Dori where she shared the key insights from her book, <u>The Couple's Retirement Puzzle: 10 Must-Have Conversations for Transitioning to the Second Half of Life</u>. As someone who has worked with hundreds of retirees over the last decade, I was so impressed with her grasp of the key issues people are wrestling with, in particular effectively engaging others who are impacted by the decisions we make in this stage of life. Her tools and tips will undoubtedly help all of us in embarking on these important conversations and being able to do them in a way that results in a positive outcome for everyone involved."

- Keith Lawrence, Financial Planning Association, Orange County, CA

"Dorian's presentation of Strategies for the Second Half of Life at the Natick Community-Senior Center this January 2015 was an inspirational, down-to-earth and personable overview of the many considerations individuals and couples can and should think about, talk about and act on for a more comfortable and easy retirement future. Dorian shared personal stories, specific examples of other's struggles and patiently answered questions. It was a wonderful, thoughtful and eye- opening evening. Thank you, Dori, for sharing your expertise.
- Sharon Kirby, Program Assistant, Natick Community-Senior Center

"Dori is a masterful coach for couples considering, or taking steps toward, retirement. Her insightful and open style sets the stage for a comfortable and rich learning environment. Both pragmatic and inspirational, she helps make sense of endings, new beginnings, and the medley of uncertainties in between. Many more important conversations are happening tonight because of Dori!"
- Patricia Smith, Managing Director, New Directions

Table of Contents

Honoring the Art of Our Lives

I met Alan O'Hare at an aging and spirituality conference in 2009.

That meeting was the start of a lovely friendship, and we've been doing work together over the years. He joined me for some of my classes on aging, and we have collaborated on a few projects. I had the absolute joy of seeing the production of some of his plays and stories and reading his book.

He has an incredible history at the Center for Community Counseling and Education and was the director of the Girls Center in Walpole, MA. He's done consultation and training, instructional design, educational media, organizational development work, community development work, and he is also a playwright and has both acted and written many plays.

I was also part of a group of which Alan was a part. We called ourselves "The Gang of Four," and we worked together and talked about helping people find their voice and finding stories that expand rather than inhibit their lives.

In this interview, Alan discusses his journey as a community psychologist, university educator, actor, playwright, and director, all woven together in his calling and artistry as a "Seanchaí /storyteller." These skills are also currently integrated into being a "curator" who highlights moments from a person's life that can be honored through the art of a story, a journal, a performance piece, music, dance, or visual art form. This model can also be adapted to the life journey of a family, clan, community, or culture.

We reach a place in our lives during the third stage when we still envision what we still seek to accomplish or discover, and part of our lives is devoted to reflections about the journey that has brought us to this point.

Alan's role as curator serves in gathering the art from a person's life through dialogue and creative exercises that will highlight significant moments of:

- Discovery
- Love
- Learning
- Challenge
- Wonder
- Accomplishment
- Joy

You can download and listen to the original recording of this interview and download the handouts here:

https://revolutionizeretirement.com/alanohare

Please note: the offer of the consultation mentioned in the recording is no longer available.

Let's get started!

Dorian Mintzer

Interview with Alan O'Hare

Dorian Mintzer: Alan, I know you as a Celtic storyteller and Seanchaí, and I'd love it if you could share some information about how you've become a curator and how you got here?

Alan O'Hare: What's gotten me here? So, many people and many blessings and a lot of people who just touch my life in special ways have brought me here. But over the years, it's been through my training and practice, but I think it's also historical, cultural, and I grew up in a tradition.

We grew up in Boston, and my family ran a boarding house, and my father was a collector of tales. I would say he was a weaver of tales. He didn't tell them, but he brought people together who told them.

I've been drawn over the years to people from all cultures who honor each other's stories. Growing up in Boston's inner-city was an excellent opportunity to meet people from different cultures and learn with them and grow.

I've always been fascinated by what people's paths were and their stories from those paths. The tradition I came from, in a Celtic tradition, is that of the Seanchaí.

The Seanchaí is the Celtic storyteller, but the Seanchaí is basically a weaver. That tradition goes back about 2500 years, and the Seanchaí spends his or her time going into villages and staying there for up to six to eight months visiting the various houses in that village. A hundred or so families would gather and listen to their stories. While listening to them, the Seanchaí would weave those tales together, and at the end of that stay, he would leave the villages with this tapestry, a tapestry that wove all their stories together.

As a psychologist, I was doing it from a different perspective, but essentially, I was trying to weave those stories together in terms of mental health. As a community psychologist I addressed the community's needs and saw the disparate stories that people brought into that community that could help with the community's healing and evolution. It was just this wonderful opportunity to be present to all of this.

The theme of mysteries and miracles were the themes that always drew me. By mysteries, I'm referring to the mysteries that Rainer Maria Rilke, a German poet who says, "I know nothing. Be patient with everything unresolved in your heart and try to love the questions themselves."

I thought that's a wonderful way to think about the mysteries and miracles. It's about learning to love the questions. Our lives are filled with questions. Often, we get worked up and anxious and fearful. When I listen to Rilke's words again about being patient with everything's that's unresolved and try to love the questions themselves, that makes me want to love and grow with all that.

The miracles are the miracles of Walt Whitman, who said in one of his poems, which was a segment of *Leaves of Grass*, " I know nothing else but miracles, Whether I walk the streets of Manhattan, Or dart my sight over the roofs of houses toward the sky, Or wade with naked feet along the beach just in the edge of the water, Or stand under the trees in the woods."

And he goes on talking about miracles everywhere. Miracles are part of everybody's experience. Part of my work over the years has evolved into trying to witness and honor the mysteries and miracles not only in my own life but in the lives of other people as well. I wanted to see what their journeys have been about, be it individuals, cultures, or communities, and what they discovered, and the tales that come from that, and the lessons they want to share.

Dorian Mintzer: It sounds like becoming the curator helps people draw out the miracles and mysteries of their lives.

Alan O'Hare: I really love going to museums, not only art museums but also museums of all forms. I've been reading about various individual curators over the past several years, and I've been really drawn to what they try to do. When they focus on a particular artist, arts group, or an art perspective, they try to find out everything about that person or group and promote it and present it in such a way that it integrates all of what that artist has to share.

They weave together all the pieces of that person's life with their art perspective. By bringing the world together to learn and be educated from that and interfacing with it, they can learn about themselves in the process.

There's another thing that's happened with curators. I've noticed that they're bringing forth not just about the artist but also about their background. So, if the artist lived in the 17th century, the curators usually weave in or integrate that period's music. They'll present historical items from that time. They'll put it in perspective.

They're continually weaving about who this artist is, what this art is, and weaving it all into life. More and more, I'm noticing that it's a celebration of the art through the weaving of all the parts of that person's life. In a way, each of us has something about our own lives, especially as we go into this retirement phase.

Our life has been a form of art, and some of the art has been quite tragic and filled with suffering and sadness, while other parts of it have been glorious and wonderful. Since we stand at this point of retirement, whether we stop working or not, it's that third age where we just turn around and look and take in all that's been taking place.

So, as a curator, I'm still a Seanchaí weaving the tales, but I'm looking at the larger perspective of people's tales and how they can celebrate that and how they can bring that together with some form that they can leave as an inheritance. Dori, you do this wonderful thing through your book, *The Couple's Retirement Puzzle*, about helping people to really look at their life story with their overall life management but also their finances.

I think it's a wonderful thing you do. What you do is you try to weave all of the person's lives as they are planning for the next stage, and you ask them, "What is it that you want to do with all of the resources that you have?" Does that make sense to you, Dori?

Dorian Mintzer: Well, absolutely. It's the reflecting, the coming to terms with where we are. I love what you were saying before about the importance of the questions to determine whether you'll be able to move forward in a new way. Can you give a couple of examples of how you've worked with people to help them

tell their story or through you, be able to tell their story? People want to know how they can use this for themselves. Can you provide some examples?

Alan O'Hare: This has come about through all my work and life experience. When I work and have written plays over the years, I've always tried to not just write about a theme in a play, but it's like, "What is everything that surrounds this play?"

I was consulting with an organization in Boston called the Massachusetts Housing Finance Agency, which serves 4500 public housing properties across the United States. They hired me as a consultant to come in and visit the various sites, and especially those sites that were having difficulty. One of the sites had to do with the community of elder housing in Lowell. They were doing quite well for a while, and then the state legislature passed a law that people with disabilities and mental illness, and other forms of illness would be integrated into elder housing. That created a lot of discord, so they hired me to go in there and see if I could work with the community and help resolve differences. One of the things that came out of it was that we decided to de-velop an educational theatre group based on the residents and with the residents.

They were eight people who were elders and eight people who had a history of mental illness who volunteered to be part of this. It was a chal-lenging experience initially because neither group wanted to talk with the other group, but they both wanted to be part of this theatre group. There was this paradoxical invitation to create this, and I remember that the way to bring them together was through conversation, but they wouldn't talk with each other.

However, one day, one of the young women spoke about her mental illness history and how it changed her life. She was in nursing school and dreamed of being a nurse all her life, and then had to leave nursing school and the career of nursing because she had a schizophrenic break and wouldn't be able to become a nurse because of that illness. Two of the elderly women, when hearing this, stood up and walked down and sat beside her and then just put their hands on her shoulder and said, "We know what you're talking about, honey. We've been there." And then they just sat with her and consoled her, and she consoled them. They had this wonderful moment together, and then everything changed. This wonderful moment witnessed this transformation taking place through them, and it wasn't because I did anything special. I was just witnessing this.

From that point on, they decided that the theatre piece they wanted to do was a story based on their lives called "Love Can Build A Bridge." It was based on the concept that they were a group that lived behind a wall of oppression and that the only way out would be that people had to share their love. This included people that lived in the community but also people outside the community. That's what they presented on the stage, and it became this wonderful production.

Over the next three years, they performed it twenty times throughout the state. They performed it at the statehouse and two universities, and it became this miraculous event. I look back now and see I also was serving as a co-curator because I was bringing together all the elements of their lives. What was the music for this play? What was the dance of this play? What was the drama of the play, and what were the colors? What were the visual arts of this piece? The audiences across the state would feel so enchanted, and the production was wonderful and quite moving.

Dorian Mintzer: What have you found are the key reasons people don't embark on this discovery journey in their life direction? What gets in the way?

Alan O'Hare: I think that there's a lot of fear about what we'll find, and I can say this from some of my career counseling clients. There's an aspect of regret. What if I find that at fifty that I wish I had been a violinist all my life? So, there's a way of protecting ourselves from that kind of awareness. What if I discover that some of the things that I, that people I admire, or relationships that I hold dear, whatever - when I take them on a shakedown cruise, they don't hold up as much as I hoped they would? There's a fear that some of our assumptions about how the world is and how we are, and how our relationships are, are not as they are. So, I think that's part.

There's that fear that time has passed us by. And to say the opposite of that, that we have so much energy for the moment now and isn't it better to choose that, to know more now so that the remaining time we have is full of life, even if we've been on restricted rations up to this point. I think that part of it is not having a framework for doing it. How do I do it? I'm curious, but I don't know how to do it.

I think the backpack is an intriguing framework to review and to also think about money and security. People have subjective money and security issues that would get in the way, and we often play them against our fears, such as, "How I'd love to be a violinist, but I couldn't afford to." "I can't go back to school, and I can't do x, y, or z and allow the money piece to answer that or the security piece to answer that," and it may be the case.

But suppose the effect of it is not to embrace the essence of it. In that case, it may cut you off from not seeing that you could study violin at an adult ed center, that you could teach music in a school setting, that your love can find transformation in some other way that doesn't cost a lot of money or maybe cost almost no money. It's more rearranging how you feel about those existing things.

So, there are no simple answers. But we can think about the concept of creative risk--that there are certain risks that we need to take in our life that are essentially life-giving or creative. And there may be some rules that we have been living in our life that are such that they prevent us from living the expanded life we want. By looking at those rules we live by and what we're sacrificing by our continuing adherence to those rules, we may be able to awaken our interest more vividly.

Dorian Mintzer: I was able to see a video of parts of that production, and it was very, very moving. I heard the dialogue between people, and it was self-reflection and dialogue with other people that helped create this story together. I know there is another example of these two women, The Circles in Time?

Alan O'Hare: Right, The Circles in Time.

Dorian Mintzer: The project, Love Can Build a Bridge, certainly involved risk-taking on the part of the individual residents, to reflect and to share. I was able to see parts...I wonder if that might be another nice example for people to hear, another way people can think about becoming a curator of their lives. I know in these cases you were helping them. Still, it's a way to think about how we can take some of what we learn and think about what we can create for ourselves. As you said before, it is part of "giving back" or a legacy and can even include other family members with us.

Alan O'Hare: Yes, it's great because these two women had each individually approached me because they had heard about my work in theatre and that I worked with individuals about helping them put together their own arts or theatre pieces or just simply writing their own stories. I've worked with several people who want just to gather all the experiences of their life and put together a book and find a theme and all of that. The book can be very small. So, these women, Amelia Kana, who was born in Italy, and Elaine Siegel, who was born in Germany, approached me individually because they had many ideas about what they wanted to celebrate, as they were very accomplished women.

Amelia was a leading fashion designer in Boston on Newbury Street, and Elaine Siegel became a world-famous psychoanalyst. Because of Elaine's history in dance, she integrated the World of Dance and Psychoanalysis, and she wrote several original seminal texts about dance and psychoanalysis. She had her own institute in Switzerland. Each of them had this rich background, but they wanted to tell the story of their beginnings, of the journey of their lives. I met with them individually about two hours a week, where they would share their stories. I would take some ideas down, and then they would go off and write more, and I coach them about their writing.

This went on for maybe two to three months, and on one visit, Amelia started talking about remembering the bombers. She lived in Northern Italy during World War II, and she remembered the American bombers flying overhead, and she didn't understand what was going on since she was six or seven years old at the time. She said to her grandfather, Nono, "Nono, what's going on?" It was a big rumbling, guttural sound up in the sky. The sky was blanketed with these planes, and she was terrified, and her grandfather said,

"Everything is safe now because they are going to bomb Germany and bomb Berlin, and the war will be over soon." Later in the day, she would hear those same planes came back, but the sound was dramatically different. It was much tinnier, and she said, "What is the story, Nono?" He replied, "Well, the planes are empty now because they dropped their bombs." This was on a Tuesday that I met with her, and she told me this story. It was very moving and very touching. She told me she wanted to tell that story and was thinking about bringing it together through music and some form of movement, not only as a story in a book, but she wanted to bring it to life on a stage.

I always met with Elaine on Thursdays. I met with Elaine that week, and neither one of these two women knew that I was meeting with the other. So, I met with Elaine, and Elaine told me she started to remember the bombing in Germany when she was in Berlin. She was six or seven years old and remembered hiding with her maid in Berlin's underground caves. She heard the bombs dropping and whistling and destroying Berlin and remembers being terrified. It was just a really shattering experience for her, and the echoes came to her that week. I remember sitting there in utter silence and not knowing what to say. So, I told her Amelia's story that she told me two days earlier from the other perspective. Elaine said, "I have to meet her." I called Amelia and asked her if she would be willing to meet. I brought the two of them together.

The following week when I brought them together, I was with Amelia, and we went over to Elaine's place and walked in. The two of them stood there for about maybe five seconds in complete silence, and then they walked to each other, and they embraced. It was like two sisters who had met, long-lost sisters. For the next two and a half hours, they sat there and talked, and I didn't say a word because they knew each other's stories from a different perspective. This wonderful, amazing experience of this revelation took place in both people and the revelation of their lives.

They decided to bring their two stories together into one form in which they named Circles in Time. It became a production piece that we performed after spending another year working on it and putting it together. Not only was it a dramatic piece with actresses, but it also had dancers and a musical element with some original music. I now look back and see it as part of being the curator. The curator is the one who brings all the elements of a theme of art to celebrate a person's life.

Dorian Mintzer: That's such a beautiful example of creating the space so people can home in on their life and then figure out how to celebrate it. That can be done by oneself as well. It does make me think that there could be a family event or maybe include other people.

Alan O'Hare: I think what you're saying that people can do this individually is true, and again, we don't always have to think that they must be highly dramatic events. Our own lives have their own drama at a personal level. I just finished a book called *Dear World* with a woman who was 93 years old at the time of the writing. She wrote letters to people that she had known and met over the years since she was in World War II. She had written six letters a week, one letter a day to people she had met and known. Each letter was six to ten pages long. She did this even when she was working full-time and raising a family.

She had been writing letters for all these years, and finally, she wanted to put together an integration of all that she had been thinking and learning because of her letters into a book. The stories are lovely and wonderful, and it's about her family and friends or people that she met and her perspective on the world. The book's title became *Dear World* because I once told her that she had written a letter to almost everybody in the world but had not written a letter to the world itself. She stopped and said, "Oh no, but I should, shouldn't I?" And with that, she sat down and wrote a letter to the world. "Dear World, I haven't spoken to you formally before, but..." She went on, and that became the preface to the book.

At age 93, she had been in her retirement for many decades, but this was her revolutionizing in some ways. With another perspective, she was able to do something with her letters, and now her family has what Meg Newhouse calls a "tangible legacy" with the book of the letters. They have this gift that will be with them for generations to come. She is quite joyous about this because she has always dreamed that she wanted them to really know who she was.

I think, in some ways, that's what takes place at this revolutionizing your retirement life stage. Okay, so, who am I? Where have I been? What am I doing, and what am I seeking to leave behind? What am I trying to celebrate about my life, and what am I trying to raise questions/concerns about my life and the world around me? It has many, many dimensions to it, and the role of a Seanchaí curator is how can I, in this case, me, be of assistance in helping to bring this together and weave these stories together. Some people hire me to do this.

I just serve as a consultant for other people, and they go out and do it themselves, and periodically they check in and say, "What do you think?" For me, what I think is that it's all wonderful. Maybe some points need to be highlighted, but it doesn't need to be done through writing. I have some people I've worked with, and they've done it all through their art, their visual art. Some of them have done it through some of their woodworking or some of their crafts that they've done.

Some of them have made afghans and wrote it on tapestries. Other people have made music and woven it together with the music of their lives. As a curator, the Seanchaí uses the tradition of bringing it all together. The question now is, how do we bring our own lives together? In some ways, that's part of what our challenge is because we feel pulled in so many different directions, ever to have the time just to take a breath and say, "Amen."

My granddaughter is always asking, "So when did you do this, grandma or grandpa?" I find a way to express that, and maybe it's through some knitting that I do, perhaps it's through some stories that I tell, it's perhaps through some art, perhaps it's through photographs. You look back at all the photographs you've taken over the generations, and then you decide to put them together in the form of a story. You don't even have to do many words; you just use them - its own little story-telling tradition. That's something I've done with people, and it's just such a wonderful way. They always just love that as well as families and communities.

The one piece that took place after I worked with Amelia and Elaine was this community of the Sisters of Saint Joseph in Boston. It's a community of nuns that began in France in the late 1700s. Two of my cousins were nuns, and I had lots of contact with them over the years. One of the sisters who taught visual arts at Regis College was really brilliant and taught philosophy and religion. She approached me (we had met a couple of times) about working on some piece. We had no idea; we were just bringing together some theme where she did a lot with the visual arts, and I did a lot with the music and story, and could we put something together. And what came out of what we created was a piece called "Songs of Remembrance in Five Seasons."

Essentially what it became was a celebration in remembrance of all the history of the sisters. It was presented in their main chapel in Brighton. We did four productions, which included a dress rehearsal. We had huge audiences, each of them about 200 people, and it was a multi-arts piece because Sister Anne Grady presented this piece as a great slideshow.

As the play was taking place, she had dramatically created visual arts of nature that tracked the storyline that was taking place between a news journalist who was interviewing this nun. All of this was taking place in the audience's presence where it wasn't on a stage; it was throughout the audience. We had actors and dancers and musicians. It was like this bulky art piece, and it just became this wonderful, wonderful piece.

This came about by weaving all of the forms together because it's one's language, not only the literal language you speak, be it in Spanish or Greek, but your heart's language, and how can you find a form to express that language? What I do as a Seanchaí is to help people discover their language or affirm their language. Many people discover them, but I affirm it and help them find a form to bring it more fully to life.

Dorian Mintzer: The photography idea is resonating with me. People could start just with some photos or family photos. What if somebody were to say, "I'm not creative in all the ways that you're talking about. I don't know how to get in touch with this." How would people begin to think about becoming a curator of their own life?

Alan O'Hare: Sometimes, the word curator throws people off. I think it is just merely reflecting and remembering. What is it that you remember that were special moments in your life? Moments that touched you, moments that changed you, and to whom do you tell that story? And sometimes, the person says, "Well, I don't have anybody to tell that story to." It's like if you could have somebody to tell it to, what would you say to them? Part of my role is to help coach them, but even if they're not going to talk directly to me, I just ask, "What do you remember?" I think that where some of us get thrown off, we think, "Okay, I have to have a beginning and a middle and an end to this story." That's not what it is; it's like you're walking through the woods, and you see things, and it's like that's a memory. You see all the birds on the bird feeder. You see the frogs in the pond; those are images, and it's just like you are saving this little collection of images.

This wonderful writer from Uruguay is called Eduardo Galliano, and the book *is The Book of Embraces* (RevolutionizeRetirement.com/embracesbook). And he writes these wonderful, wonderful stories about his life experiences. Each story does not exceed one page, and they're just these wonderful stories. I mean, it's just simple -- he just tells what he remembers. But it becomes this enchanting journey through his life, and it could be as simple as that -- learning to write the alphabet.

Dorian Mintzer: These are beautiful examples, and I'm so glad you said that people sometimes hear the word creativity, and they cringe. There's this creative spark in all of us if we let ourselves open to, just as you say, what we see if we're taking a walk.

Alan O'Hare: That's right, because we're the curator of our lives. This meaning curator comes from the word "to care for," so we are the ones who care for our lives. When we reach this point of retirement, that's where we decide how we want to care for our lives now. It's like, the way I care for my life is I think of my children and my grandchildren. What is it that they want from me? And I think of myself -- what I want is to remember back.

I didn't know my grandparents because both my parents were born in Ireland. So, I never had an opportunity to meet them. I have a couple of pictures of one set of grandparents, and I look at them, and I want to somehow step into that picture and say, "Grandma," and then I just want to ask her a list of questions. I want to talk to Grandpa, "Grandpa, can you show me around and take me places?" And it's that kind of thing.

It becomes, "What are the questions that the people of your life want to share? What are the memories of those special people from our lives, and what are the things of them that you remember that you would like others to remember about them?" For example, it's like there was a good friend I had, you never met him but let me tell you something about him. And that's what the story is. It doesn't have to be a quote "about you"; it's about these special people that you met along your journey, and you're sharing the journey story.

The history of the Seanchaí is the Seanchaí was always going someplace, and I think of myself very much that way. I love just going to different places. In the past five years, I had an opportunity to meet the different sisters from Rwanda who survived the genocide and were very much leaders during the genocide. They have been coming to the greater Boston area to live here for a while as they go for graduate school. I was fortunate to be introduced to them. I've been meeting with them when they are here and just hearing their stories, and they go back to Rwanda and are doing programs with which I've talked with them. They're weaving them into the school system, in the educational systems. They're becoming curators for the children even though they are not retired. They're creating forums in which the children can remember their lives and honor their stories and honor their perspectives and honor the art and bringing it to life, and it's wonderful. It doesn't have to be, "This is a story about me." It's about the things I've seen.

I look out right now, out of my window, as I'm sitting here talking with you. I'm looking out the window of my office, and my partner, Pat, has made this wonderful labyrinth in our back yard, which is right in the shade now. And the labyrinth is made up of all these stones, good-sized stones but the stones are from different places in the world. For everybody we know who travels somewhere, she gives them an assignment to bring back a stone. I'm sure customs people are wondering what's going on here. We have all these stones from Morocco and all over the world, Spain, and Greece. The story is out there. The story is everywhere, and it's like, how do I want to remember it? How do I want to share it?

Dorian Mintzer: And how do I open the space just to notice what's around me and realize that at every step of our journey, there's some miracle. And parts that we sometimes overlook, like just thinking about it and thinking about the stories and images that inform me, make me who I am, and help me connect with people. That could be a way to begin.

Alan O'Hare: Yes, I think of my father and mother who ran a boarding house, but they also worked full-time jobs. They would come home, and my brother and I would help set the table, and then the boarders would come in, and my mother would cook the food, and my father would help and do all these things. After dinner was over, especially in good weather, the two would go into the garden. My mother loved the flower garden out front; my father loved the vegetable garden out back.

Sometimes, they'd be helping each other, which is after a day's work and taking care of the boarders. I'd look out the window with my brother and see them be so content because they were in the earth. They weren't just gardening; they weren't digging up the soil; they were in the earth. Neither wore gloves when they were gardening, but the image for me is their hands in the earth. And so that's part of them. That's their story and one of the wonderful stories that I think of as well. It's often the simple things that we remember.

During one of our earlier interviews, Dori, it was in the air on the phone and I'm a visual person. I remember the experience of thinking of it as being in an Irish village on a misty day when you can't see the other person, but then the rain would clear, and you would hear a voice there it would be. You couldn't see them very well, but you could listen to their voices and their breathing. You could sense the community because we're all part of the community. We're all part of their lives, including those moments of loss. We think, "I don't want to think about that," or "I don't want to talk about that." How do we honor that as well and create the space for that?

There's a wonderful musician, Dave Matthews of the Dave Matthews Band, who wrote a great song in 2011 called *Space Between*. It's about that - it's about the space between. In each of us, there's that space between. It's like, what is that space between that person I love? What does that look like? What does that sound like? What does it feel like? What's the energy of that? How would you describe the space between you and your mother, you and your father, you and your brothers, you and the world, you and the walk in the woods? What's the melody? What's the color? What's all of that, and then that's the story, and that's where it begins.

So now I'm standing here looking out the window at the labyrinth. Another part of me is walking down the road on the west coast of Ireland, waiting for the boat to go over to Deer Island, where my father was born. The mist is in my face at the same time, and I'm thinking, "How can I be in two places at the same time?" Because when many of us are in two places at one time, like while we're driving into the city and listening to something on the radio and something's going on here, we get our cell phone going, and we're in four places at the same time.

Dorian Mintzer: Multitasking is what many of us frequently do in the world.

Alan O'Hare: Multitasking is part of our consciousness, too, and it is part of that dance and that circle. It makes me think of younger people, like our children and our children's children, because it's a different life experience for them. There's that space between us but a very different space between them and what we experience as a space between them. What does that sound like and look like? If they revolutionize our retirement, we will revolutionize the retirement of people 50 years from now. How does that change?

This is a great opportunity, and our lives are now in that place of our stories. It's where it is, like what films are about and what movies are about. It's about all that, just taking the tales, right?

Dorian Mintzer: It's the evolving of our lives -- it's the transforming, the paying attention, the opening the space. Maybe what you were saying before was tied into the losses or the changes in the "what's next of life?" Noticing what the feelings are or what the images are or deciding how to remember an event.

Alan O'Hare: That's right. I recently did a presentation for some retirees in Walpole and asked about where the stories were. I said to them, "Look at your hands -- just hold up your hands in front of you. Not just at the palm of your hands, but just slowly revolve your hands so that you can see them from the side angle. Look at the back of your hand and look at all dimensions of your hand. As you look at your hands, these hands are filled with stories. So many people have touched these hands, and they touched so many things and people. Each hand may be like an injury that was part of the hand, or something else may be about the hand. Those hands have applauded; those hands have held someone else's hands."

There are so many dimensions to the hand, like what you can do with a hand, or what has this hand touched that just gave the fullness of life. I remember the first time I touched my son and then my daughter's hands. I just reached out, and they grabbed my finger and, I can see them holding my finger at present. I can feel my son's feelings at one time and then my daughter, and the first time they each held that finger.

The feeling was just - I still don't have language for it. I've asked myself how to express that, and I'm still at a loss of how to express it or describe it fully. I think it must be a piece of music somewhere, some notes or some images, or maybe it's unexplainable. When I look at this finger and hold it up separately, that's what there. It is very small hands holding that hand, holding that finger, and a story and a poem. There's a dance, right?

Dorian Mintzer: That's beautiful. Looking at my hands and thinking about how it just resonates with all the people it's touched. It's true -- there's poetry in all of us if we open to it.

Alan O'Hare: And the revolutionize the retirement is about that; it's about being at that moment where we've done all these things. It's a moment of pause. It's like it's a moment where we come to this oasis and we stop, and somebody at the oasis says, "So where have you been? Where have you traveled?" And I respond, "That's a great question. I've traveled to many places." And they reply, "What's come to mind? What do you remember from your travels?" So, you sit there in this oasis, and then you begin to remember where you've been. It doesn't mean you are not going to do other things and accomplish other things.

I have more plays inside me and more music inside me, and more dance inside me. There are times I just want to sit here and remember where I've been, like when I visualized my finger being held by my son's and my daughter's hands. That's enough for now. And that's what revolutionizing retirement is because it's not just for me -- it's not just for me so that I can speak. It's for those who travel around beyond us. It's like my grandparents in Ireland who have been gone for 75-100 years, but I want to look back and say, "I remember you."

It's like when we revolutionize our retirement. It's not about memories, nostalgia, or perspectives. It's about the way you see the world and the way you think of the world. It's your mind also, not just the world of emotions. It's your mind and the world of your thoughts. It's the way you think and see and breathe and the way of your opinions, what you want to share, and what you want people to remember. It's like asking, "What is life? What have you learned on the journey that you want those behind you to remember?" It doesn't need to be your grandchildren. It can be just somebody, just the world.

It's like this woman, Mary, when she wrote *Dear World*. She wrote, "Here are some of the things I'd like to share with you, and here are some other thoughts I have." I think she wrote a section on things that needed attention and correction, so she gave the world a couple of instructions on what the world had to do better.

Her children loved that, too, because whenever the children visit with her, she always gives them these wonderful loving words of advice. So, she gave the same thing to the world, some loving words of advice. "You're doing a pretty good job, world, but I think you can pay more attention to this. I think there are a few too many wars going on. I don't know what you can do about it, but I just want you to know that there are too many wars going on right now. A lot of people get hurt, so what's the future." Some of it really cut right to the core.

Dorian Mintzer: That is a beautiful example. It makes me think of the gestalt approach when

Alan O'Hare: Or make a list of your questions and have a dialogue with each of the questions, right? Here are ten questions that have been bothering me for several years now. You're at this point in your retirement and make a list of the questions and say, "I'm not going to write a book. I'm not going to create an art piece." Just think what it is you want to say to that question. Maybe a piece of art comes out of it, perhaps a story comes out of it, or perhaps it's just some-thing that happens in your life that you use as a dialogue with some other people. It's taking time and just pausing a little.

It's coming to the oasis and just stopping. We don't have to judge - oases don't have to be drive-throughs. I know we have a lot of drive-through places on the roads now. We can stop at some of these places too and just sit there and look. I remember doing some teaching in San

Jose, New Mexico, several years ago. It was my first morning there, about 6:30 or 7:00 in the morning, and I was standing on the street corner. I didn't know where to go for breakfast. This old beat-up truck pulled next to me, and these three guys were sitting in the front seat. They were farmers from the country, and having lived in the city, I was thinking, "I'm in trouble now." One of them came up and said, "You look like you're lost." And I said, "Well, I'm just trying to figure out where to go for breakfast."

And then we had this conversation that lasted maybe five or seven minutes about where to go for breakfast. This is them just stopping because they saw this guy standing there looking like he was lost. I think, "Who are these people?" I don't know who these people are, but I remember that moment about them, and I can still picture their faces as they have this animated conversation about where to go for breakfast. And they get back on their truck, and I thanked them, and we shook hands as they parted, I thought, "Wow, that's really cool, right?"

Dorian Mintzer: What if people start to curate and find that they are in over their heads and need to pull back? What happens if the process becomes too powerful -- it sounds creative and interesting but then lands people in places they hadn't anticipated? How do you help people get out of the hole?

Alan O'Hare Before getting into the hole, let somebody else know that you are deciding to take on this venture so that they are a person with whom you can touch base in your journey. That's one way, and I recommend having a life-line as I have. I get into something many times, and I just call my friend Richard and tell him what I've been working on and that I got into some-thing very powerful and I'm not sure where to go. Richard listens to me and tells me I might need just to put it aside until it comes up again, and he'll give me a call, and we'll talk. You have a liv-ing coach who's a friend. They don't have to do anything per se, but they comfort you, support you, and nurture you while you're going through it.

Dorian Mintzer: It is part of the important step. Each of us is special and unique in our own way, and hopefully, we recognize that it takes a village, and we're part of a community. I think the importance is being able to do this with other people.

Alan O'Hare: Walt Whitman would say, "I know nothing else but miracles." So, whoever you are, take a look out wherever you are, breathe, and have nothing else but miracles.

You can download and listen to the original recording of this interview here: https://revolutionizeretirement.com/alanohare

Please note: the offer of the consultation mentioned in the recording is no longer available.

BONUSES FOR READERS

As a gift for my readers, I have an amazing retirement resources list for you.

Get your copy today at

http://10KeyRetirementIssues.com

ABOUT ALAN C. O'HARE

Alan C. O'Hare is a community psychologist, university educator, actor, playwright, and director. He's both a Celtic storyteller and a Seanchaí storyteller. Alan has an incredible history at the Centre for Community Counseling and Education. He was the director of the Girls Center in Walpole, Mass.

He's done consultation in addition to training, instructional design, organizational development work, educational media, as well as community development work. He is a gifted playwright and has both acted and written many plays.

He is the author of *Love, Mary B: A Teacher's Gift*. (https://revolutionizeretirement.com/lovemary) His mantra is: "It's always a beautiful day in the neighborhood."

Website: www.lifestorytheatre.org
Email: bridges95@aol.com

ABOUT DORIAN MINTZER

Dorian Mintzer, M.S.W., Ph.D., BCC (Board Certified Coach) is a coach, therapist, teacher, and writer with extensive clinical experience. She speaks to professional and community groups. As a coach, she helps women, men, and couples reinvent themselves in the second half of life.

She is the owner of Revolutionize Retirement, co-founder of the Certified Professional Coaches Retirement 20.0, founder of the *Boomers and Beyond Special Interest Group*, and founder and host of the 4th Tuesday *Revolutionize Your Retirement to Create a Fulfilling Second Half of Life* interview series. She weaves holistic life planning, adult development, and positive psychology into programs that tap and shape clients' energies into roadmaps for wiser, more enhanced living.

She has written about many topics pertaining to the second half of life and aging. She is co-author of *The Couples Retirement Puzzle: 10 Must-Have Conversations for Creating an Amazing New Life Together*. She's been featured in various media such as the *WSJ*, *NY Times*, *USA Today*, *Washington Post*, NPR, *ABC Evening News,* and the *Today Show*. She delivered a TEDx talk called, *Embracing your Bonus Years: A Time to Grow, Learn and Evolve*.

Website: https://www.RevolutionizeRetirement.com
LinkedIn: https://www.linkedin.com/in/dorimintzer/
Twitter: https://twitter.com/dorianmintzer
Boomers and Beyond Special Interest Group:
https://revolutionizeretirement.com/bandbsig/
Revolutionize Your Retirement Monthly Interview Series: https://revolutionizeretirement.com/interviews-with-experts/

OTHER BOOKS BY DORIAN MINTZER

Co-Author

https://revolutionizeretirement.com/crpbook

Contributor

https://revolutionizeretirement.com/65things

https://revolutionizeretirement.com/randr

https://revolutionizeretirement.com/livesmart

https://revolutionizeretirement.com/65thingstravel

https://revolutionizeretirement.com/6secrets

https://revolutionizeretirement.com/mothersretirement

https://revolutionizeretirement.com/70things

https://revolutionizeretirement.com/80things

https://revolutionizeretirement.com/oob

https://revolutionizeretirement.com/rightsource